of Life

Volume I

Aspects of Life

Volume I

H. Croston

Paper Doll

Published by Paper Doll
Belasis Hall
Coxwold Way
Billingham
Cleveland

ISBN: 1 86248 084 2

Typeset by CBS, Felixstowe, Suffolk
Printed by Lintons Printers, Co. Durham

To my wife Annette,
for her caring, her love
and for being there.

CONTENTS

'EVACUEES' (1941 – 1945)

Being evacuated when you are eight years old,
Is not hard to comprehend,
Just rethink the memories,
From the beginning to the end.

Two young lads from Liverpool,
Heading out of town,
Masks and bar of chocolate,
But not knowing where you're bound.

We ended up in 'Highley',
A village near Bridge North,
To escape the German bombers,
And the atrocities of War.

Not knowing our fate or destiny,
We had to stand our ground,
And waited until selected,
By a local female hand.

Her name was Mrs Walker,
She said you call me Nan,
But this lady was no substitute,
For the person we called 'Mam'.

Life was a game of survival,
Competing with the rest,
The local village children,
And countryside and all its pests.

1

We didn't have many comforts,
Or solace when in pain,
Especially when potato picking,
In the . . . rain.

We survived the mumps and whooping cough,
And goose grease on your chest,
But scabies between your fingers,
That really was the test.

A boil on the bum was something else,
That no one could explain,
And then a Kaolin poultice,
Just to relieve the pain.

When the war was ended in 1945,
I can look back in retrospect now I'm 65,
We have lots of happy memories, my kid brother
       and me,
It wasn't all bad, being an Evacuee!!

Dedicated to Robert Spruce and Family

MEMORIES OF BEING EVACUATED
SEVEN POEMS

BIRD WATCH

Cherries ripening on the trees,
Behind the Kings Arms pub,
Two young lads beat a corrugated sheet,
To ward off the birds from above.

PEA PICKING

Pea Picking was labour intensive,
You had to pick quite a lot,
To fill a sack,
Would almost break your back,
Just for a few to end up in a pot.

POTATO PICKING

Potato picking was the worst,
Off all the tasks we performed,
In the wind and the rain,
Aching all over with pain,
All you wanted was to be warm.

Then riding home upon a truck,
Sitting on your bucket,
You sing and sway,
And reflect on the day,
And curse the stability of the bucket.

PIG'S DINNER

Collecting peelings for the pig,
Was not a pleasant job,
It had to be done,
Regardless of the hum,
And the occasional bite from a dog.

Our chariot was a chassis of a disused pram,
With a bath tub for a container,
Patched up with a tin without Spam!

We called at all the houses,
Asking for food for the pig,
The wheels they would whirl,
As we sped everywhere,
For we had a very fast gig!

COAL DELIVERY

Coal was delivered at the garden gate,
Then the work was begun,
To get it to the cellar,
Took two little fellas,
More than an hour to shift a bloody ton!

You would carry each bucket more than twenty
  yards,
Each step engrossed in pain,
It was no use complaining,
Even when raining,
For the next load would just be the same!

GOING TO CHURCH

To go to church on a Sunday,
Really was quite a treat,
With no jobs to be done,
Only hymns to be sung,
And the occasional treat or a sweet.

I still have my presentation prayer book,
Awarded when I was eleven,
The message it told,
Was very bold,
Your reward will be in heaven.

QUIET MOMENTS

The view from our bedroom window,
Was tranquil and serene,
The golden corn,
On a summer's morn,
And the changing patterns of green.

The Clee hills in the distance,
They seemed so far away,
With your thoughts of home,
You were never alone,
And the war would end one day.

I trust you enjoyed my recollections,
In my life as an Evacuee,
In a village somewhere,
In Shropshire,
A place called Highley.

'REFLECTIVE THOUGHTS' (1941 – 1945)

Highley was a village,
A refuge from the war,
A place they sent young children,
Three score or more.

Adaptation was the lesson,
For each and every one,
Look to your survival,
The battle had begun.

No frills or nice surroundings,
Things were rather bleak,
No hot and cold running water,
Or toilet, with a moving seat.

We lived our lives on a daily basis,
Each one was a test,
To outwit the other person,
Because you knew that you knew best.

Looking back in retrospect,
We did have lots of fun,
Making your own amusement,
Laughing at the little things,
Like a boil on your bum.

GOLDEN YEARS (1948 – 1998)

I started work in forty-eight,
Serving my time, I thought, would be great,
Served right through to fifty-four,
'A time served sheet metal worker' – who could
  ask for more!

National Service, my next call,
Royal Engineers, had me a ball,
Egypt, Cyprus, in the Middle East,
A rottweiler police dog, what a beast!

Next two years,
Worked very hard,
Got myself married,
To my sweetheart.

Now had a wife,
And then a son,
The years ahead,
Meant lots of fun.

Seventy-two brought to an end,
A period of life when I lost a friend,
My dear wife, forty years of age,
Departed this life to an earthly grave.

In seventy-four, picked up the threads,
Married Annette, no regrets,

Gained myself another son,
A new mum too, for number one.

Now I've come to ninety-eight,
Time to reflect and contemplate,
Our Silver Wedding is shortly due,
My golden years, have silver too!

THE VISIT

My favourite trip is to my local tip,
To dispose of all my rubbish,
The skips all there,
Are never bare,
For with rubbish, you can't be snobbish!

I fill my car to capacity,
I do not waste the space,
With weeds from my garden,
And black bags of kitchen waste.

Arriving at my destination,
I speedily unload,
With the knowledge that another 'landfill',
Will benefit from my load!

NEW BRIGHTON

Going to New Brighton,
Is not what it used to be,
All the fun of the fair,
That's not there,
Or the ferry across the Mersey.

The promenade is bright and breezy,
On that I must agree,
But I fill with despair,
As I stand and stare,
Where the bathing baths used to be!

It's nice to have recollections,
Of things that used to be,
But when they're
Not there,
And look at reality!

HOUSE FOR SALE

Due to disenchantment,
And matters beyond our control,
The decision has been taken,
It's time to sell our home.

To get away from the city,
And the hefty council tax,
The environment and discontentment,
And attitudes so lax.

To seek a peaceful haven,
Of contentment and repose,
A home in the country,
Among the fields and hedgerows.

To achieve our retirement ambition,
The sign went up today,
'View by Appointment'
We are on our way!

PARENTS

All of us have parents,
On that you must agree,
The life they have given,
Is unique to you and me.

So make the most of your life,
This precious commodity,
Use it, don't abuse it,
This human rarity!

HOUSE SEARCHING

To go house searching creates quite a stress,
Between two people looking for the best,
In terms of finances and probability,
Set against reality.

You seek and find and then compare,
Of what you want and what is there,
The truth at all times will prevail,
Continue the search, time will avail,
Your expectancies on the house search trail.

EDNA AND STAN

Edna is a friend,
Who lives in Hesketh Bank,
Her loving husband Stan,
Has joined 'The Eternal' bank!

Had their electronic business,
In a town called Ormskirk,
Supplying all the electronic bits,
For things that did not work.

Stanley made an organ,
From a self-assembly kit,
Putting it all together,
Gave him quite a kick!

Edna did the cooking,
While Stanley made a noise,
While trying to impress her,
With his acoustic, electronic poise!

The organ now is standing,
In the living room,
Waiting for someone to make it vibrate,
Around the room.

I lift the lid, then select a key,
To play a simple tune,
Edna came in smiling,
'That reminds me of our honeymoon'.

FACT OR FICTION

Estate agents have a language,
And a jargon of their own,
When it comes to describing property,
Or a potential home.

Their interpretation,
Or should it be misrepresentation,
Of fact or fantasy,
Leave you to wonder, do they deal in reality.

In need of 'slight updating',
Leaves the mind agog,
This short phrase of assumption,
Could cost you a few bob!

The garden is slightly overgrown,
Would baffle many a grower,
But those who live in this real world,
Would be reaching for a flame thrower!

The rising damp is 'slight',
Yes to a level beyond compare,
'The woodworm is treatable',
Or the cost of a set of stairs!

My advice to all you agents,
Describe what the buyer has seen,
Not what belies reality,
Or is it just a dream!

EYESORE

Walking to the paper shop,
All I see is lots of 'grot',
Paper and litter all around,
Half eaten take-aways on the ground.

Weeds between the paving slabs,
Dogs that foul with their pee and dabs,
All this has happened in my home place,
All because of animals, some called 'The Human
    Race'!

I have to recourse to sell my house,
To get away from all this scouse,
To find a home in a locality,
Where 'animals' have some respectability.

MY GARDEN

I sit here in my garden,
Letting the world drift by,
Watching Mucus Nimbus,
Drift across the sky.

Watching birds feeding,
Under our pine tree,
Looking at plants and flowers,
And the joy they bring to me.

And when my days are over,
I wonder where I'll be,
Probably in some garden,
Under a rose tree!

THE APPOINTMENT

Sitting in out-patients,
Waiting for the Doc,
Wondering by chance if the little finger,
Has fallen off his clock.

Getting very fidgety,
Getting very bored,
People talking pace-makers,
And not being able to walk!

At last the nurse calls my name,
She says, wait a minute,
Oh sorry love, go over there,
You're in the wrong clinic!

PAIN RELIEF

I wake up in the morning,
Sometimes before dawn,
Experiencing pain all over,
Arthritis heralding another morn!

To get relief you have to move,
Mobility is the cure,
Flex the muscles, release the joints,
It's time to hit the floor.

A call to Mother Nature,
Replenish with a cup of tea,
Sit down and write some poetry,
That's relief to me!

THE DENTIST

A visit to the dentist,
Can be quite traumatic,
But when you're there,
And in the chair,
Fear renders you static.

You anticipate the beginning,
You're praying for the end,
Now the treatment's done,
And your bum is numb,
Your denture becomes your best friend!

HAIR TODAY

Going to the barbers,
Is not what it used to be,
This once male bastion has become encroached,
By the hands of femininity!

No more talk of unions,
Or the match you did not see,
Of your hopes and aspirations,
Or what you're having for tea!

But like so many other things in life,
I think you must agree,
The female hand is much softer,
When fitting your toupee!

LOOKING AT HOUSES

Looking at houses can become quite a bore,
Viewing all before you,
From ceiling to floor,
Noting main features,
Like the wood block floor!

Listening to the small talk,
Of achievements great and small,
Like building a garage,
And a loo in the hall.

Deciding this place is not for you,
Regardless of the new sani-loo,
Off to see another,
The usual ruse!

AULDENE GARDEN CENTRE

This Garden Centre is supreme,
To all the others I have seen,
It has an elegance of its own,
A feeling of contentment as you roam.

A delightful array,
Of plants and shrubs,
Ornamental pots,
And flowers in tubs.

A vast display of products and wares,
From slug repellent to tables and chairs,
From bells and chimes to hammocks that swing,
Auldene Garden Centre has everything.

A restaurant with a conservatory,
That invites you in for coffee or tea,
An ambience of its very own,
Just like eating a buttered scone!

Croston Conservatories are located there,
But there's no connection with the name I share!!

DANIEL

Daniel is a seven year old boy,
But quite a big lad,
The pride of his Grandma,
The first grandson she's ever had!

She loves that boy,
He brings her joy,
In her life he is supreme,
Nothing else brings her more happiness,
Than when Daniel's on the scene.

She'll say, 'Come here, give me a hug,'
But Daniel hesitates,
Their arms entwine,
Just like a vine,
Daniel is 'just great'.

FAMILY

Being the youngest member,
Of a family of eight,
Gives you an advantage,
To sit back and contemplate.

You can start at the very top,
That would be Mum and Dad,
Then work right down the ladder,
To the next to youngest lad.

First I have two brothers,
One is at 'eternal rest'.
The next one is still with us,
He is full of zest!

Then I have two sisters,
One is 'up above',
The next lives in Nottingham,
Quite near to Robin Hood.

Next came three brothers,
Harry, George and John,
The previous two have left us,
But the latter lingers on.

That just leaves yours truly,
I trust you will agree,
That the youngest in the family,
Upholds the family tree.

THE ROAD OF LIFE

Life is but a journey,
Travelling through time,
Not knowing which direction,
Destiny will define.

But if you face that journey,
With happiness in mind,
The road that leads to fulfilment,
Won't be hard to find.

And when on that road to fulfilment,
Be careful how you tread,
For the journey you will travel,
Will last until you're dead!

THE LOST HOME

The scene from my bedroom window,
Is one of devastation,
The house once there,
Is now laid bare,
Right down to its foundation.

The bricks, the mortar and the rubble,
Are strewn across the ground,
This place once known,
As someone's home,
Will never more be found!

THE ROAD

Driving along the highway,
With a white line as your guide,
The reality of living can be measured,
As a ten centimetre divide.

Staying on the right side,
Of that white divide,
Requires your concentration,
Just to stay alive!

You put your life at peril,
When trying to overtake,
If the road's not clear,
Then you are near,
To a ten centimetre, life or death mistake.

FLAT VIEW

We went to look at flats,
Advertised in the press,
But on reaching our location,
I really felt depressed.

The building looked impressive,
The price was quite good too,
But the scene from the lounge window,
Made it a home 'without a view'.

The tatty looking neighbourhood,
The general demise around,
The first impression scenario was,
Let's be homeward bound!

MY CAR

My car to me is my mobility,
When I am racked with pain,
To perceive a need,
And travel indeed,
Regardless of wind and rain.

The joy I receive, travelling with ease,
Words cannot explain,
But it takes the load,
On the open road,
Motability my happiest gain.

FINANCIAL GAIN

By doing the lottery twice a week,
My fortune I am trying to seek,
But my numbers never appear,
On the screen bright and clear,
My numerical powers are weak.

But I will try until I win,
Then I can cancel my personal pin,
To this end I must persevere,
Until one day my numbers appear.

LOVE

Love is an emotion,
That we all sometimes feel,
Sometimes it is tender,
At times can be surreal.

Love is everything,
To each and everyone,
Love can be fantasy,
It's there and then it's gone!

Love is what you make it,
Each and every day,
Love is all our tomorrows,
For the past has gone away.

So if you do love someone,
Be sure to let them know,
For love without communication,
Is a love they will never know.

CIRCLE OF LIFE

Life is but a circle,
Going round and round,
Just like all the planets,
In their heavenly abound.

To measure life's capacity,
Of all creatures great and small,
Would be an endless equation,
Like the infinity and wonderment of it all!

So don't take life for granted,
It is a special gift,
Utilise its powers,
And minimise your drift.

LAUREN JESSICA

Lauren is a little girl,
Very special to me,
A little girl whose very being,
Is there for all to see.

Her dark blue eyes,
Her dark brown hair,
Her smile, her cheeky grin,
Her impish ways,
Make happy waves,
The moment she enters in.

I love this girl so very much,
I would have loved her as my daughter,
But destiny decreed this to be,
My very first 'granddaughter'.

INFLICTED

My arthritis overtook me,
After I had broken my neck,
In an accident not of my doing,
My car a total wreck.

To overcome this burden,
Of the pain within my spine,
I keep a sense of balance,
Between my body and my mind.

MOMENT IN TIME

If the words of a song tell a story,
Then the music must keep it in time,
To remember the lyrics and the music,
Is to recall a moment of time.

Each one of us has special moments,
We keep in the back of our minds,
For the songs they are there,
For the memories to share,
And bring back that moment in time.

SHANDY

Shandy was our household pet,
A four legged friend,
With a tail at one end,
And a face you could never forget!

Her disposition was friendly,
Her nature was pure gold,
But show her a cat,
And that was that,
To hell with a nature of gold.

We gave her to a new family,
For nature was taking its toll,
On those that cared,
Who no longer shared,
The energy of that wonderful dog!

THE UNIFORM

A baseball cap and trainees,
A tracksuit in two-tone blue,
A tee shirt advertising something,
Is this the modern you?

Age is no distraction,
Between boy and man,
The uniform of all athletes,
Is part of a conceived plan!

So here's to all the athletes,
That frequent pubs and clubs,
You won't receive gold medals,
But be permanent athletic subs!

LADY GREEN GARDEN CENTRE

Lady Green,
Oh Lady Green,
As a Garden Centre,
You are supreme.

Your delightful array,
Of plants and shrubs,
Your ornamental pots,
And flowers in tubs.

Your vast display of products and wares,
From green fly killer to a garden chair,
From bells that chime to hammocks that swing,
Lady Green has everything.

The coffee room and all its charm,
The aromas there create a crazy balm,
The sandwiches and all the cakes,
The gourmet cuisine has what it takes.
Your pavlova is beyond compare,
Oh Lady Green,
I'm glad you're there!

Dedicated to the management and all the staff.

HOLIDAY EXIT

We had to cancel our holiday,
Due to illness of my wife,
All the planning and the bookings,
Just faded like a light.

The build up to our departure,
Was only days away,
But the doctor's diagnosis,
Confirmed we had to stay.

Cancelled our hotel booking,
And the ferry too,
Contacted holiday insurance,
Not much else to do!

MEMORIES

Memories are pictures,
Created in your mind,
By a sudden thought or impulse,
That your brain can't leave behind.

Each picture tells a story,
Of an event that was in your life,
Be it whole or partial,
A memory cannot always suffice.

Memories come in categories,
Good, evil and bad,
Heartache, love and laughter,
How you think about them,
Depends on being happy or sad!

So when you search your memory,
To recall a point in time,
Remember life that's passed you by,
For tomorrow could be borrowed time.

NUMBERS

Our life is governed by numbers,
From the time we are born,
Be it early afternoon or evening,
Or at the crack of dawn.

The time and date are recorded,
To give identity,
To another human person,
Whether it be you or me.

So when you are celebrating,
You own personal anniversary,
Recall the date life came your way,
For it's yours till eternity.

RETIREMENT

My wife and I are retired,
Now we are sixty-five,
A lifetime still before us,
It's good to be alive.

We survived the German air raids,
We survived the Asian flu,
With a given strength of character,
There's nothing you can't do!

The boys are in their thirties,
The grand-kids, they're just fine,
With a lot of hope,
And survival 'without dope',
We can go on until the end of time.

'A CUDDLE'

A cuddle is for someone,
Who thinks others do not care,
A cuddle is for someone,
At the time of their despair.

So give someone a cuddle,
And let them know you care,
That life with all its frailty,
Is there for all to share.

'EGOTISM'

There are people in this world,
Whose 'ego' is beyond compare,
They've seen it all and done it all,
There's nothing left to compare.

But if you let your ego,
Dominate your life,
The comparisons you cannot match,
Will cause you trouble and strife.

So instead of being egotistical,
Just try being sincere,
Then your journey on life's highway,
Will be one without fear.

'FRIENDSHIP'

It was back in 1945 our friendship did begin,
Two twelve year old lads,
The pride of their dads,
With nothing to lose but to win!

We shared each other's hobbies,
We shared each other's joys,
We didn't stand on sorrow,
We were just two happy boys.

We developed an attachment,
From mutual esteem and respect,
From boyhood into manhood,
The bond has not broken yet.

So here's to my friend and our friendship,
Now fifty-two years have passed,
The pleasure's been mine, for this pal of mine,
Has given me memories that will last.

*This poem is dedicated to my friend Alf, in memory
of all we stood for, in respect of one another and
mostly of our friendship.*

Alf Thomas Glaysher
Born 24/12/32
Died 04/09/97

GORGEOUS GEORGIA (25-6-97)

Today is Georgia's birthday,
She is one year old,
A bundle of joy and affection,
A treasure to behold.

Her blonde fair hair,
Her bright blue eyes,
Her total sense of being,
Are reflected in the awareness,
Of this little human being.

This is the second little girl,
That fate has bestowed on me,
For this is my number two grand-daughter,
Who smiles and laughs at me.